Tastes of Greek Islands
SANTORINI

Myrsini Lambraki

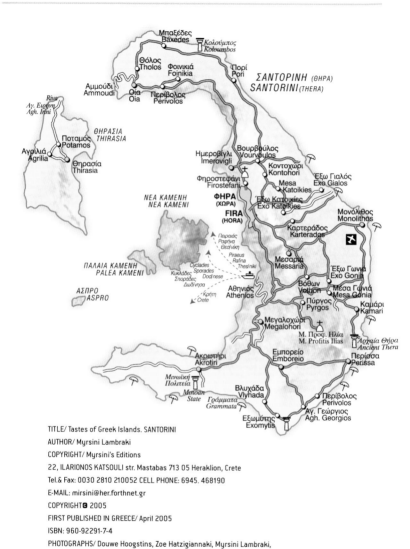

TITLE/ Tastes of Greek Islands. SANTORINI

AUTHOR/ Myrsini Lambraki

COPYRIGHT/ Myrsini's Editions

22, ILARIONOS KATSOULI str. Mastabas 713 05 Heraklion, Crete

Tel.& Fax: 0030 2810 210052 CELL PHONE: 6945. 468190

E-MAIL: mirsini@her.forthnet.gr

COPYRIGHT© 2005

FIRST PUBLISHED IN GREECE/ April 2005

ISBN: 960-92291-7-4

PHOTOGRAPHS/ Douwe Hoogstins, Zoe Hatzigiannaki, Myrsini Lambraki,

FOOD STYLING/ Spiros Mprilakis

TRANSLATION/ George Trialonis

LAYOUT/ MKS Advertising Tel.: 0030 2810 341986

Table of contents

SANTORINI:
A VIBRANT ISLAND

In the very ancient times the island of Santorini was known as Strongyle (the Round One), owing to its particular shape. Ages later, and by dint of its natural beauties, its name was changed to Kalliste (the Gorgeous One) – perhaps by the Argonauts who landed on the island en route to Colchis (see Golden Fleece). Again, at a later time the Lacedaemonian settlers renamed the island to Thera, after their leader. As the centuries wore on the island of Thera took the name Santo-Erini by Italian sailors, who crossed the Aegean on their way to the Holy Land and called at the island for supplies. Since the island was rather inaccessible then, the Lacedaemonians anchored at the cove of Therasia where, a few meters from the beach, nested the chapel of Saint Irene (Santo Erini in Italian). Repeated reference to this "haven" in association with Thera resulted in a new name for the

island – Santorini (the letter E was dropped) – which has survived to this day.

The island of Santorini is a unique place, suffused with energy, memories, history and mystery. It is now laced with a gray coastline, the result of past volcanic action. The sparse beaches are teaming with guests in summer. The light blue church domes are emulating the turquoise of the sea, while thousands of residential windows overlooking the Aegean or patches of vineyards and vegetable gardens. Santorini is a unique place because it offers an extraordinary variety of natural light, colours and aromas. Furthermore, if you take a stroll in the midst of vegetable gardens, you will be amazed by the variety of their produce. In a land that is seemingly barren you will find white baby aubergines (sweet like honey), currant tomatoes (acescent in taste) and split-peas, which is famous all over Greece.

In terms of cuisine, the island is famous for its tomato-balls and the refreshing white wine produced from local grape varieties. Grape harvesting by the end of August is more like a festival, involving the participation of the entire population of the island. The grape varieties cultivated on the island are: mandilàri, asàrtiko and aidani. Using sun-dried currants the locals make sweet puddings which, along with melitinia, stuffed cookies (koulourakia) and kopania represent the 'patented' sweets of the island.

Travelers
of the past

This dry island, which owes its existence to ancient volcanic action, exerts a peculiar charm on people. The imagination of those who have only read or heard about it oscillates between the blue-green of the Aegean and the ash-gray of the rock that forms the land. Those who have visited the island, images of magnificent sunsets, of the mysterious fog the veils the Caldera rock, the sensation of sweet local tomatoes, the crispy freshness of the asírtiko wine and the full-bodied taste of the vinsanto wine shall remain with them for many years. But let us look at the comments that travelers to Santorini made two or three centuries ago.

At a time when traveling at sea was more like an expedition, there were brave souls who defied the perils at sea with the aim to educate themselves in local customs, products and morals.

French Jesuit Francois Richard visited the island of Santorini in 1644 and wrote comments about the anhydrous cultivations and products of the island: "This island produces barley of excellent quality, large quantities of beans, while there is a kind of seed that the locals call pea and the Italians favetta...

"The staple of the locals is a kind of hard bread which is made from barley and comes out very hard. Part of the wine production on the island is sold directly to the isle of Chios, to Smyrni and occasionally to Constantinople.

The wine production today is excellent and the bulk of it is transported to Chandax of Crete by boat."

CAPERS

The caper flowers are the summer 'roses' of the Mediterranean. You can see them hanging from the southern crevices of the Caldera rock and from the white-washed walls of old Cycladic houses.

The ancient Greeks were familiar with the caper plant, and we have plenty of references in ancient texts where the authors comment on the merits and use of the plant's buds. In antiquity capers were used as appetizers or as condiment. Zeno's often quoted exclamation 'by caper!' shows the significance of this plant in antiquity. The Byzantine Paul of Aegina recommends a slice of bread topped with capers, vinegar and honey as an appetizer before each meal.

In modern times capers are basically used to spice a variety of dishes and sauces. This is mainly due to their very small size and particular taste. Collection of the caper buds should be done preferably in the months of May, June and July. The capers are collected when they are still the size of a small bean and placed in fresh water for 10 days. To turn the capers sweeter, the water needs to be changed often. Subsequently, the capers are placed in a solution of vinegar and salt and sealed in air-tight glass jars.

Pickled capers are good for 10 days. This mode of preserving caper buds (and leaves) is common around the Mediterranean basin. The same is true as regards the use of capers as a pungent supplement to various salads (e.g. tomato or even cabbage).

The caper buds and leaves are unique, offering a piquant taste and freshness even when dried.
They find extensive use in the local cuisine of Santorini. Capers marry well with and add a pleasing colour and taste to chick-peas puree, tomato salads, and chick-peas balls.

SPLIT PEAS PUREE: FAVA, YELLOW AND RARE

The term originates from the Latin Favus, meaning fava beans. The ancient Greeks produced a wholesome meal out of the dry fava beans.

The split-peas of Santorini are famous all over Greece. This is not only owing to their delicious taste when pureed, but also because they cook fast, relative to other varieties.

The split-peas of Santorini are more like green peas (albeit golden-yellow in colour), which in the old days were reduced to powder in hand mills. The split-peas of Santorini constitute a basic ingredient for other dishes. The yellow puree that results from the boiling of split-peas marries well with tomato sauce, capers, onions, meat, octopus and such herbs as mint and parsley.

The split-peas of Santorini are rather expensive, and this is because of their advantage in cooking, excellent taste and flexibility in a variety of recipes.

Local production amounts to 4-5 tonnes annually.

COD FISH AND GURNARDS ON THE GRILL

Owing to the ragged and steep-crevices coastline, the majority of the inhabitants of Santorini resorted to agriculture, the cultivation of volcanic earth, and less with fishing. Fish was mainly imported, particularly the salt cod. Soon cod became very popular among the poorer people, not only in Santorini, but in all the Aegean islands. In Santorini you can try a version of the Portuguese Brandada de Bacalao, cod cooked in the oven with strong, creamy garlic sauce. Mr. G. Hatziyiannakis, an expert in the Santoriniot cuisine and owner of a restaurant ('Selini') recommends the 'Psarolia' (air-dried alevins on the grill or in the oven), and skate with garlic sauce. On this island the shore dinner (kakavia) is delicious, particularly with a bottle of local red wine.

If, perchance, you find yourselves dinning at "Ta Dihtya" in the village of Perivolos, you could order an assortment of gurnard fish on the grill or the grouper cooked in sea water in a clay vessel.

CHLOROTYRI (a cheese variety)

This is a local cheese variety of very limited production, which you will not find anywhere else in Greece. It is a white, creamy cheese with a tinge of sour taste. It is made from goat's milk and can be spread on slices of bread or mixed in the Santorini salad (cherry tomatoes, rusks, lettuce and anchovies).

Instructions: strain the milk through a fine tulle or old pillow-case. Heat the strained milk (do not let boil) to pasteurize. Add rennet (a natural enzyme obtained from the stomach of young cows), approx. 1 teaspoon per 100kg milk. The milk coagulates within 10 minutes. Transfer it to butterfly muslin to let drain the whey. What remains in the muslin is the chlorotyri, which you strain lightly by hand in a strainer. Sprinkle with a hefty amount of salt and cover it with a piece of linen cloth. It is ready for consumption 24 hours later.

WHITE & PECULIAR

A white aubergine! Yes, this is a unique vegetable with alabaster look and excellent taste. It is surprisingly sweet, with very few seeds. You can slice and fry it or chop it up raw in salads. It does not absorb much oil when fried.

APOCHTI

This is the center loin of pork. When processed or cured, this pork can be used in recipes several days later. To use it, first clean and rinse it well under tap water. Then sprinkle it with salt and let it stand to drain for 2 hours. Subsequently, you can soak it in strong vinegar for three days, then strain and cure it following three stages:

Firstly, treat the meat with ground cinnamon and place it in a strainer for six hours. Next, treat it with savory (chopped) and let it rest for at least six more hours. Finally, treat it with a mixture of black pepper and a little cinnamon. Let it rest for 6 hours and then rig it in a safe place to air-dry well. When the meat hardens a little, it is ready for use. Cut thin slices and serve, or use it in other recipes. It marries well with chick-peas puree accompanied with tomato sauce (blend the tomatoes with spring onions in vinegar and oil sauce).

SANTORINI CHERRY TOMATOES
A VEGETABLE THAT NEEDS
NO WATER TO GROW.

This tomato species was a rather late arrival on the island. It was first introduced in 1850. It is small, bright red in colour and slightly flat on the sides, with an acescent taste. This species adjusted well to the volcanic terrain, the strong winds and the high temperatures.

It also adjusted to the dry conditions of the soil. This vegetable sustains itself with the meager quantities of water the humid summer nights can avail. The water vapours are stored in the ground and in the leaves of the plant.

Years later, other tomato species

flourished on the island: a more hardy species from the isle of Kos (which is sweeter than the Santorini cherry tomatoes), and the bournela, another variety the size of a small egg with an acute sour taste.

Currently the Santorini cherry tomatoes are

cultivated only in limited garden patches, while the output is standardized by the local Agricultural Association and the "Pavlo-Petrou Economou Co.".

These tomatoes are seeded by the end of February and the seedlings are thinned in April. Subsequently, they are transplanted and the fruit is collected by mid-June.

The Santorini tomato-balls (pseftokeftedes) are made from the mashed flesh of this fruit and taste delicious. You can find the Santorini cherry tomatoes in the form of canned tomato paste, which is ideal for giouvetsi recipes. Also, the same vegetable, if sun-dried and stored in jars with olive oil, can be used in spaghetti recipes and other dishes.

Why the Santorini
cherry tomato is one of a kind?

It is a bushy plant which bears small fruit with thick skin, emulating in size the cherries. The soil it grows is also unique: dry, volcanic earth. The result of this combination is a sweet and mildly sour fruit infused with the aromas of a season long forgotten. The unique vegetable is cultivated, processed and packaged with extreme care by the last remaining factory on the island of Santorini. You will find it in all major supermarkets or vegetable outlets either as is, canned or as tomato paste and juice. The Santorini cherry tomato is ideal for cooking as it allows superb possibilities for exceptional tastes.

The old folks on the island of Santorini claim that the seeds of this tomato species originated from the Suez Canal, where Greek sailors tasted the fruit and liked it so much that they decided to bring seeds of the same back to Santorini. The seeds flourished in a soil that was as dry as that of Egypt.

To sustain the cultivation of this tomato species the R & D department of the Union of Theraic Products has plans for a pilot project involving experimental cultivation of cherry tomatoes in alternative soils applying new techniques. Soon, this tomato will come under the distinctive title PDO (Protected Designation of Origin).

Initially, the processing of the Santorini cherry tomatoes was more of a family affair. However, in 1915 mechanical processing started in small factories established on the island. Before the earthquake of 1956 there were 11 such factories for processing and canning of these Santorini tomatoes.

WINE

There is evidence to support the claim that viticulture and wine making on the isle of Santorini is about 3500 years old. In the process of excavations at Akrotiri location, archaeologists discovered the blackened remains of kindling from burnt vine stalks. They also discovered grape pits in vases, as well as jars with floral paintings representing bunches of grapes, and a plethora of vessels, e.g.

stirrup jars used for storing liquids, particularly wine.

These findings lend credit to the claim that there existed wine trade activity in Santorini during the prehistoric period (ca. 1700 BC).

Viticulture in Santorini is the oldest in Greece. Hence, one could surmise that vines on the island are probably autochthonous, which can be supported by the fact that the Santorini vineyards have never been struck by the phylloxera pest. Actually, the Santorini vines are among the few Europeans of the self-grown species. It is very likely that the resistance of the local vines to pests and diseases is the result of the islands physical constitution in volcanic soil.

The old autochthonous vines, averaging a life-

span of 60-70 years, grow in arenaceous soil poor in clay but rich in volcanic ash.

VINE TRELLIS "BASKETS"

If you visit Santorini in Spring or Autumn, provided you can get away from the enchanting beaches for a few hours, take a brief tour of the island's interior. You will not fail to

notice that the vineyards are lined with "baskets", i.e. coils of vine trellises rooted to the volcanic soil and rising at a height that, from some distance, look like wicker baskets lying abandoned on the ground.

However, at the bottom of those "baskets" shoot roots deep into the soil. The vine trellises are very much alive, waiting for the sign of Spring to shoot eyes, and the hot breath of summer to bring forth precious bunches of grapes.

This "basket weaving" was started by the local farmers hundreds of years ago, in an effort to protect the grapes from the strong north winds (meltemia) of August. Now, it seems that the vines are trained to run a circular path round the stalk, and the result is a natural basket where grapes grow safely.

Irregular masonry structures, basically heaps of stones, are erected to provide additional protection to vineyards against wind erosion. Terraces from volcanic earth are built for the same effect, but also host patches of vineyards.

The vineyards of Santorini have evolved to require little water, as much as they can capture from the water vapours of the fog that covers the island in August. The water is trapped in the soil and the leaves of the plant.

This unique microclimate of the island has a considerable effect on the grape varieties grown and on the quality of the wine produced.

WINE GRAPE VARIETIES

In the beginning of the previous century approximately fifty wine grape varieties were cultivated on the island of Santorini. Currently, there are only thirty. The most popular white varieties are: Asírtiko, Athíri, and Aidáni. The equally important red varieties are: Mantilari, Mavrotràgano and Voudómato. The Athíri and Aidáni grapes are cultivated in small quantities, but give excellent, aromatic and full-bodied wines.

Other white grape varieties are: Aetoníchi, Critikó, Potamisi, Rozakí, Savatianó and Aspromoschàto.
Other red grape varieties are: Roùsso, Moschàto, Rodítis, Fràoula and Aetoníchi. The black grape varieties are: Nychàto, Eftàkilo tis klimatariàs, Saríki and Mavróthyro.

Asírtiko: This is the prevailing cultivar of Thera. It found purchase in the volcanic environment of the island to evolve into one of the most impressive varieties of Mediterranean vineyards.
This variety gives approximately 80% of total grapes produced on the island. The asírtiko variety produces one of the best white wines in Greece, distinguished for its high acidity and full-bodied aroma.

Athíri: This is an old variety grown on Crete and known for its thin skinned and aromatic grapes.

Aidaní: This is a rare variety producing highly aromatic grapes used in antiquity to produce the "Apiranthos" wine of Naxos. The aidaní grapes are blended to add aroma to the Vinsanto wine.

The most famous wines produced in Santorini are the Nychteri (white wine), the Asírtiko and the Vinsanto. The former, Nychteri, took its name from the fact that farmers would harvest the particular vines until late at night (Gk. Nychta), when the temperatures dropped and toiling in the fields became bearable.

SUN-DRENCHED GRAPES FROM THE DEEP OF THE CENTURIES

"But when Orion and Sirius are come into mid-heaven, and rosy-fingered Dawn sees Arcturus, then cut off all the grape-clusters, Perses, and bring them home. Show them to the sun for ten days and ten nights: then cover them over for five, and on the sixth day draw off into vessels the gifts of joyful Dionysus." Hesiod, Works and Days, c. 700 BC.

This is a recipe by Hesiod for the production of sun-drenched wine. In antiquity the sweet wines were known as "οίνοι πάσσοι" (vinum passum). Wine varieties differed in terms of modes of vinification, which was a factor of geographical location. All wine production shared a basic process: following collection, the grapes were spread under the sun to lose half of their weight by dehydration. Subsequently, they were transferred to wine presses for the collection of must in pithoi (large clay jars) for fermentation. Occasionally, mature wines were added to the must in the pithoi to thus add aroma and character to the new wines. This process of vinification produced wines that were aromatic and high in alcohol, which necessitated their dilution with cool, fresh water. In keeping with the name change of Santorini, this sweet wine, too, changed its name from "Thera" (Lacedaemonian) to "Santo-Erini" (Italian).

As mentioned earlier this sweet wine was also referred to as Vino Santo or Vinsanto (i.e. the sweet wine of Santorini) in the Middle Ages. The name Vinsanto was more sonorant, and also identified the origin of the wine to buyers around the world. Initially, it was exported to Constantinople, Chandax (modern Heraklion), Chios and Smyrni. At a later time, when Venice became a major marine power in the Mediterranean, this honey-like colour and aromatic wine conquered the markets of Venice, Trieste, and Ancona and other destinations that the ships of the Most Serene Republic called at.

Thus, the Vinsanto was in great demand for the banquets of the nobles in the Middle Ages.

At the same time it became indispensable among travelers, not only by dint of its rich taste, but also for the fact that it could act as a rich source of calories, invigorating the body to withstand diseases and hardships that long and precarious navigation entailed. Enologist Mrs Kourakou-Dragonas found a reference to this Greek wine in contracts executed between the Venetian Republic and crews of sailors. The stipulation read that the wine was to be "administered" to the crew before breakfast. The Vinsanto was quite hardy, in the sense that it could endure long trips without going bad, which was considered an additional advantage for exports.

The Vinsanto represented the most lucrative business for the isle of Santorini. The particular viticulture became dominant, displacing all other cultures, on the island. The Kioutsouk-Kainartzi Treaty (1774) paved the way for the Vinsanto to conquer the Black Sea region. By the end of the 18th c., and up to the first quarter of the 19th c, the bulk of the Vinsanto production was exported to Russia, where it was also used for Communion in the Orthodox Churches.

However, the golden age of exports started to take a plunge in 1840, and never recovered until the beginning of the 20th century. This decline in Vinsanto exports was attributed to a radical restructuring of the international wine markets during the 19th century. More specifically, the taste of consumers changed dramatically following technological developments that facilitated the marketing and exports of competitive wines at great speed, relative to the previous centuries. The high price of the Vinsanto was also implicated for the demise of its exports. Prices were high on account of the geographical and terrain constraints associated with the particular viticulture on the rocky and rather inaccessible island. However, adjustments were made in the cost of production and in meeting the particular demands of the markets, in addition to upgrading the quality of Vinsanto.

No sooner than demand for quality and brand name wines started to increase in the domestic market, did Vinsanto producers of Santorini start to reorganize production, bottling and marketing.

Following ten years of efforts, the Union of Theraic Products Association acquired full rights over the Vinsanto brand produced from the sun-drenched grapes of Santorini and Therasia. Now, the wine is under the Protected Designation of Origin, thus fully protected against E.U and third country competitors (EU regulation 753/2002, list B, 29 April 2002). This regulation has been in force since its publication in the Official Journal of the European Communities (4-5-2002).

Using a different process of production, the Italians produce a kind of sweet wine (vino santo) from other wine grape varieties. The European Union allows the use of the term vino santo on the labels of designation of origin (DOC) Italian wines on condition that the term is supplemented by the geographical name, e.g. Vino santo di Damberella. Thus, the vino santo term, initially indicative of the Santorini wine made from sun-drenched grapes, lapsed to a general (generic) designation of sweet wines.

VINSANTO:
A wine for
connoisseurs

Just pour yourselves a glass of Vinsanto wine and simply look at it. Try to appreciate the hues as they change from golden yellow to orange to the Aegean turquoise and blue. Now, taste it carefully – as would a connoisseur: notice the complex aromas, the rich taste and exceptional balance.

This is truly an aromatic wine which is counterbalanced by the acidity of the Assyrtico grape component. There is no doubt that the Vinsanto's aroma is unique as it brings forth tastes of juicy citrus fruits, the sweetness of ripe figs and raisins, of plums and hints of cinnamon and vanilla.

You may attempt to explain its sweetness, rich aromas and long aftertaste. Well, given that all good things in life require time, dedication and love, so does this "sacred" wine. The constituent wine grape varieties have long been embraced on this mysterious and legendary land, flourished on Santorini's volcanic earth and loved by the local growers and wine makers.

Following the toilsome vine harvesting in the scorching heat of long summers, the particular grapes are strewn on steaming residential roofs under the Aegean skies. It does not take more than 15-20 days for the grapes to dry completely.

Subsequently, the shriveled fruit is surrendered to the expert hands of wine makers to be processed, with the sweet juice fermented in oak barrels. Fermentation lasts for several months, until Christmas, when it stops by itself, without the addition of alcohol (this explains the label: Vin Naturallment Doux). This wine needs at least 24 months maturation in oak barrels to acquire its exceptional bouquet. The wine comes out in high sugar content (at least 90gr/lt), velvety taste and proof between 8-10.9%, depending on sugar percentage in the must. The yield is rather small: approximately 10kg of sun-dried grapes yields 2.5lt of Vinsanto.

Having concluded this brief tour in the production process, let us return to more practical matters – taste and pleasure...

The way to enjoy a glass of Vinsanto wine: just take a good sip, close your eyes and let it engulf the sense organs of your mouth. Suck a little air through the mouth before swallowing the wine. This will enhance the sensation. This wine loses nothing of its excellent features during a good meal and marries well with dried fruit and mature cheese.

Currently the isle of Santorini produces 15 types of Vinsanto wine which you can find in the wine shops of the island, Athens and most major towns of Greece.

UNION OF ASSOCIATIONS OF THERAIC PRODUCTS

The Union of Associations of Theraic Products – Santo Wines – was established in 1974 and currently is counting 2500 registered members. The Union combines business and social objectives ranging from support to its members to protection of the Santorini vineyards and unique wine grape varieties.

The Research & Development Department of the Union participates in research projects with the aim to upgrade the Santorini wines. To this end, it has organized a plants nursery of select vine seedlings to protect the VQPRD zone of Santorini from the introduction of lower quality propagation material.

The Santo Wines Winery

To better protect this invaluable fruit of the Theraic earth, the company Santo Wines set up a state-of-the art winery with a capacity to handle 5.000 tonnes of grapes in 1992. The facilities were built in keeping with the particular characteristics of the terrain, i.e. in a terraced fashion.

The Santo Wines Tourism Centre

In 1992 the Santo Wines established the Wines-Tourism Centre - an exhibition facility - n an effort to promote the famous traditional wines of Thera. Each year the Centre receives over 40,000 visitors from all around the world.

The Wines-Tourism Centre is located at the "brow" of the Caldera rock commanding a magnificent view of the volcano. Visitors are given a guided tour to the Santo Wines winery and the opportunity to taste the excellent wines while enjoying superb sunsets.

The WINES-TOURISM CENTRE offers:
• Guided tours to the Santo Wines winery to familiarize guests in the wine making processes – from grapes reception points to bottling.
• Orientation to the wine maturation cellars where one can experience a unique environment, where the oak tree barrels interact with the wines in maturation.
• Wine-tasting opportunities: experienced enologists reveal the secrets of wine making and wine-tasting to visitors who taste such select varieties as the Asyrtiko, the Nychteri and the traditional Vinsanto.

In addition to select wine varieties, the Wines-Tourism Centre has set up a special hall where visitors can find collector's vials for storing wine, books and other items relating to wine as well as a display of other products of Thera, e.g. split peas, cherry tomatoes, capers, blackberry syrup, etc.

Address: Pyrgos Santorini, 847 00,
Tel: (22860) 22596, 25128, 25420,
fax (22860) 23137
Athens Branch : 95 Platonos Street,
104 41 Athens,
Tel./Fax: (210) 5153485
E-mail: info@santowines.gr
www.santowines.gr

SIGALAS WINERY

This is a small winery located in the plain of Oea. The owner, Mr. Paris Sigalas, is very meticulous about the cultivation of the Assyrtiko, Athiri, Aidani and Mandilaria grape varieties. Six wine types are currently produced, three of which are the result of organic cultivation. The Sigala wines are characterized by their balance of a range of aromas and tastes.

During the International Wine Challenge competition in May 2004, the Sigalas Chateau won (bronze medal) the label SIGALAS VINSANTO Protected Designation of Origin for the Assyrtiko-Aidani Crop 2001.

Wine-Tasting Schedule:
April - October: Mon-Fri: 10:00 - 19:00 & Sat-Sun: 11:00-19:00

Sigalas Winery S.A.
Santorini Street, 84702
Tel: 22860-71644
Fax: 22860-71645
www.sigalaswine.gr
E-mail: sigalas@otenet.gr

BOUTARI WINERY

The Boutari vineyard is located on Santorini (or Thera), the most famous island of the Cycladic insular complex. It is property of the Boutari company and can be found on the way to the "Faros", outside the village of Akrotiri. This land, imbued in history and legend, with a rich cultural background, bears the indelible effects of the volcano — a permanent terrestrial feature – that erupted ca. 1500 BCE. The Boutari vineyard occupies an area of approximately 60,000 square meters.

The planting of the seedling roots started in 1992 to complete two years later. The wine grape varieties selected were mainly native to the island, e.g. Asyrtiko, Athiri and Aidani. Some experimental varieties were also planted in soil of volcanic constitution at an altitude ranging from 105 to 140 meters. With an eye to the quality of the raw material (the fruit) and in harmony with the environment, only 250 seedling roots were planted per one thousand square meters. The vine trellises are trained to develop in the shape of wicker baskets.

The local Boutari Winery facilities, featuring a characteristic white dome, started operations in 1989. Its role in the development of vineyards and wines on the island is considered very significant. The winery is open to the public for guided tours, offering also a wine-tasting galore

involving a wide range of Santorini wine varieties combined with projections of historical and cultural information inside the dome. The top wine of the Boutary Estate on Santorini is the White Selladia, a wine emanating the luminescence of the Aegean Sea.

A Tour in the Boutari Winery involves: a guided tour to the production facilities and underground cellars - projection of historical and cultural information - a wine-tasting galore involving 3 typical wines: Santorini Boutari, Kallisti, Vinsanto Boutari.

Following this very instructive tour the guests are initiated in wine-tasting from a range of wines accompanied with other products of the land. New, old and experimental wines not found in the market can be purchased, as well as books and other items relevant to wines and vineyards in general.

OPERATING HOURS:
daily from 10:00 to 19:00

Winery Director:
Mr. Petros Vamvakousis
Address: Megalochori of Santorini
Telephone: 22860 81011
Fax: 22860 81606
E-mail: santorini.winery@boutari.gr

CANAVA ROUSSOS
AT A GLANCE

quality from the island's select varieties: Asyrtiko, Athiri, Aidani, Mandilaria, Mavrathiro.

CANAVA ROUSSOS, the oldest traditional winery of Santorini, was established in 1836 to produce high quality wines uniquely expressing the characters of a plethora of Theraic wine-grape varieties. Decades of experience have passed on from one generation to another to find expression in the art of wine-making on this island. The characteristics of this art are: continuity, consistency and absolute respect for tradition.

Canava Roussos

With due respect to tradition, the Roussos' scions (now 4th generation) are making use of modern technology with the aim to create unique wines in terms of taste and aroma

Today, the Canava Roussos company, faithfully adhering to the island's traditions, takes advantage of modern technology with the aim to create wines with individual tastes and bouquets, using grapes of the highest

Yiannis Roussos and partners are the warmhearted hosts of visitors to Santorini every summer. They guide them to their traditional winery, the CANAVA ROUSSOS, located at Episkopi-Mesa Gonia on Santorini, to initiate them to the secrets of the unique tastes of the Theraic products and to wine tasting from a range of 8 product varieties:

Vinsanto Roussou, Santorini Roussou, Rivari Roussou, Caldera Roussou, Athiri Roussou, Mavrathiro Roussou and Nama Roussou.

For more information on the guided tours to the CANAVA ROUSSOS, and related events taking place from Spring to Autumn, please contact Mrs. Agapi Roussou at:

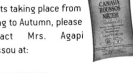

CANAVA ROUSSOS
WINES OF SANTORINI
www.canavaroussos.gr
E-mail: info@canavaroussos.gr
Main oficce: Episkopi
Mesa Gonia, ZIP. 847 00 Santorini
Tel.: 22860 31349, 22860 31278
Branch: 22,
Zisimopoulou st.,
P. Faliro, ZIP 175 64
Tel.: 210 9400017,
Fax: 210 9416699

WINERY KOUTSOGIANNOPOULOS

The vineyards, the winery (Volcan Wines) and the wine museum of Santorini are situated in the area "Vothonas"

nary puppets are used, as well as sound effects and other gadgets, to provide visitors with a very interested guided tour. In a specially decorated room the visitor can watch a film about the history of Santorini from 1500 BCE to modern times.

Wine tasting also takes place and visitors can enjoy the quality wines of this winery.

on the way to the Kamari Beach.

It is a small family business, established in 1880 from brothers Gregory and Dimitris Koutsogiannopoulos. Nowadays and four generations later, George Koutsogiannopoulos is the new owner.

Wine-production takes place in a traditional and functional building which has an impressive and unique natural cave wine museum, 6 meters underground and 300 meters long.

It presents the history of wine and the life of the wine producers in Santorini from 1660 to 1950. Moving and statio-

Daily from 12:00 to 20:00.
GEORGE
KOUTSOGIANNOPOULOS
WINERY & MUSEUM
(on the road
to Kamari Beach)
FIRA SANTORINI CYCLADES
847 00 GREECE
Tel & Fax: 22860 31322
Fax: 22860 22300
E-mail: volcanwines@waterblue.gr
www.waterblue.gr

KOSTAS ANTONIOU WINERY

Mr. Kostas Antoniou is a man of passion. There is an ancient winery in the settlement of Megalochori - representing an age-old (3500 years) local vinification landmark - which this man has set his mind to revive.

In this historic location Mr. K. Antoniou has built new facilities for production and maturation of wines. There is also a hall used to exhibit representational art and for concerts, a traditional Greek coffee shop, jewelry exhibition and for the organization of wine-tasting events.

Visitors to these facilities will have the opportunity to enjoy a tour to underground wine-fermentation halls and cellars.

Megalochori, Santorini
Tel.: 22860 23557 / 23824

AMPELONAS GAVALA WINERY

Megalochori, Santorini
Tel.: 22860 82552

KANAVA S.A. WINERY A. ELIOPOULOS

Megalochori, Santorini
Tel.: 22860 81796-7
Fax: 22860 81798

HARIDEMOS HATZIDAKIS VINIFICATION

Pyrgos Calliste, Santorini.
Tel.: 22860 32552
Fax: 22860 28395

BRIEF GASTRONOMIC LEXICON OF SANTORINI

BRANDADA: Dry-salted cod fish, soaked in water and cooked in the oven in red garlic sauce.

PSAROLIA: Small fish, mainly alevins.

TYRAVGOULO: A special way of making casserole rabbit. It involves a rich sauce made from eggs, cheese and wine.

PSEFTOKEFTEDES: Meat balls made from grated anhydrous cherry tomatoes (Santorini species) and other ingredients, e.g. grated vegetable marrows, chopped mint, parsley, oregano, dill, etc.

FAVOKEFTEDES: Vegetable-pulses balls made from split-peas puree, fresh spring onions and mint.

PSARAKIA TOU VOUNOU: Sweet aubergines fried and dressed with a lot of tomato sauce.

PECHTE APO PSARI: easy to make and quite common on the island – a fisherman's meal in the Cycladic complex. You will need fatty fish (conger eel, moray eel, or grouper). Boil in a moderate amount of water to get the right constitution of fish jelly.

SCHIZES: black and hard rusks made from local barley flour.

POULAKIA: stuffed marrow leaves.

POUTINGA: fluffy dessert made from semolina and eggs. It is served with a sauce made from sweet Vinsanto wine.

KOPANIA: a kind of "fontan" made from crashed barley rusks, sesame and raisins.

MELITINIA: small pastries resembling miniature oil lamps. They are stuffed with soft cheese and mastic.

KOUFETO: spoon dessert made from sweet pumpkin, honey and almonds.

KOLOKYTHERI: a kind of pie filled with sweet, grated pumpkin, cheese and honey.

KATSIA: a kind of pie ("skaltsouni") scented with orange rind. This is made during the religious festival of "Apokreo".

SANTORINI SALAD

(serves 8 -10)

Ingredients:

10-15 Santorini cherry tomatoes cut in halves

4-5 fresh, finely cut lettuce leaves

2-3 garden rocket leaves

1 medium-sized rusk cut to bites

1 small-diced onion

4-5 olives

1 anchovy cut to small pieces

1 tbsp caper

1 tbsp ricotta cheese

(you can replace it with myzithra)

2 tbsps olive oil

Salt

Freshly – grounded pepper

Preparation:

1. Place half the rusk bites at the bottom of a large bowl and top them with the finely cut lettuce, the cherry tomatoes, a pinch of salt, the onion and the rocket.

2. Add the rest of the rusk bites, the caper, the olive oil and the cheese.

3. Let the salad rest for about 10 minutes and then serve.

TOMATO BALLS
(serves 8 -10)

Ingredients:
3 large & ripe tomatoes (with the skin)
or 1/2 kilo of Santorini cherry tomatoes
2 onions, large and finely chopped
2 spring onions, finely chopped
1 tsp mint or parsley, fresh & finely chopped
1 tsp baking powder
2 tbsps flour
1 1/2 cups olive oil (for frying)
Salt
Pepper

Preparation:
1. Cut the tomatoes in half and deseed them. Put them in a blender and turn the switch on and off 3-4 times. The idea is to cut the tomato halves to small pieces without reducing them to pulp.
2. Transfer the blended tomatoes into a strainer and let them drain for about an hour.
3. Empty the blended tomatoes into a bowl and mix them with the onion, mint, baking powder, salt, pepper and the flour. The mixture should be thick, add some more flour if necessary.
4. Pour the olive oil into a deep non-stick frying pan and heat it. Place as many tablespoons from your tomato mixture as your pan can accommodate.
5. Fry the tomato balls over high heat until they are lightly browned on both sides. Repeat the same process with the rest of the mixture.
6. Remove the tomato balls using a perforated spatula and place them on a dish lined with absorbent kitchen paper. Serve them warm.

OMELET WITH MARROWS & TOMATOES

(serves 6)

Ingredients:
2 medium-sized ripe tomatoes, finely chopped
2 vegetable marrows, medium-sized and chopped to rings
6 eggs
4 tablespoons olive oil
salt, pepper

Preparation:
1. Fry the marrows in the olive oil. When done, drain them from the oil and add the tomatoes. Stir and simmer for 7-8 minutes.
2. Whisk and season the eggs, then pour the mixture over the marrows-to-matoes.
3. Simmer the omelet over low heat. Stir 2-3 times using a wooden spoon.

POULAKIA GEMISTA
(STUFFED MARROW FLOWERS)
(serves 6)

Ingredients:

20 vegetable marrow flowers

1 cup rice

1 large tomato, grated

1 large onion, finely chopped

2 marrows, grated

2 tablespoons parsley, finely chopped

$1/2$ cup olive oil (for the filling)

$1/2$ cup olive oil

$1/2$ lemon, the juice

a pinch of cumin

salt

pepper

Preparation:

1. Carefully open the marrow flowers, remove carpels from inside and hard stems from outside.

2. Wash flowers under tap water and place them upside down in a bowl to drain excess water.

3. Prepare the filling: use a bowl to mix in the onion, grated tomato and marrows, parsley, rice, salt and spices. Add the olive oil allocated for the filling and mix the bowl contents by hand.

4. Pick a marrow flower and place a teaspoon of mixture inside it. Do not fill flowers completely as the rice absorbs water and expands.

5. Fold the flower tops to seal in the filling, then place the stuffed flowers in a shallow and heavy-bottom pot.

6. Pour $1/2$ cup of olive oil, the lemon juice and $1/2$ cup water (perhaps less) over the stuffed flowers.

7. Simmer for 3-35 minutes then remove pot from heat and let it stand for 10 minutes before serving the meal.

SPLIT-PEAS PUREE AND CAPERS, STEW
(serves 6)

Ingredients	1 1/2 tbsps caper (salted or in vinegar)
2 cups Santorini split peas	1 tbsp white wine, unresinated
1/2 cup olive oil	Salt
1 ripe tomato, peeled and diced	Pepper
1 small onion, finely grated	

Preparation:

1. Clean and cook the split peas in a pot with 4-5 cups of water over low heat until they turn into a thick pulp.

2. Transfer the pulp into a blender or vegetable mill and run the blender/mill to turn the pulp into a thick cream (puree).

3. Prepare the caper sauce as follows: use a pot to sauté the onions in olive oil for a couple of minutes. Before adding the capper into the pot, rinse it well under tap water. Sauté the caper in the pot for 2-3 minutes; add the tomato, the wine, a pinch of salt and the pepper. Cover the pot and simmer for about 10-15 minutes.

4. Transfer the split peas puree on a platter. Using a spoon, make several wells in the center of the puree to pour the capper sauce in. Serve immediately.

SPLIT PEAS, PUREE
(serves 8-10)

Ingredients	little salt
1/2 kg split peas	little olive oil
1 small onion, finely chopped	little lemon juice

Preparation:

1. You can buy split peas in bulk or in standard packets. In any case, rinse the split peas under tap water and drain them. Bring them to a boil in a pot with 1 lt of salted water. Strain and rinse under tap water.

2. Replace the split peas into the pot with 1 lt of fresh water. Boil them until they absorb all water. Before you take the pot off the ring, add the onion and salt.

3. When the split peas are done, transfer them into a mixer bowl and run the mixer to make a paste out of the split peas (fava). Serve the fava topped with a little olive oil and lemon juice.

4. (Optional: you may sprinkle the fava servings with finely chopped onion and/or dill.)

SPLIT- PEAS PUREE "PANTREMENI"

(serves 4)

Ingredients

1/3 -2/3 teacup extra virgin olive oil

1 teacup Santorini split peas (previously cleaned, rinsed and drained)

1 medium-sized onion, finely chopped

5-7 teacups water

Salt

Black pepper, freshly ground

1 tsp oregano, dried

2-3 tbsps vinegar, from red wine

For the sauce:

1/3 teacup olive oil

3 large onions, halved and then sliced

2 medium-sized ripe tomatoes (grated) or 2 tbsps tomato paste diluted in 3 tbsps of water

1/2 tsp cinnamon, grated

1 bay leaf

Salt

Black pepper, freshly ground

Preparation:

1. Sautè the onions in a large pot with 1/3 cup of olive oil over low heat for 6-8 min. Stir until the onions soften all over. Add the split peas in the pot and stir well for about 1-2 minutes to mix with the olive oil. Add enough water to top the split peas about 5 cm above level. Cover the pot and bring the split-peas to the boil over moderate heat. Lower the heat, uncover the pot and simmer for 1 $^1/2$ - 2 hours, stirring occasionally to prevent the split-peas puree from sticking to the sides of the pot. While simmering, make sure that there is always enough water to turn the split-peas into puree. So, add water as required.

2. When the split-peas turn into puree, take the pot off the heat, sprinkle the puree with the salt and pepper and stir in the oregano and the vinegar. Cover the pot with a towel and let it stand for about 1-2 hours.

3. In the meantime prepare the sauce: Heat half of the amount of olive oil in a large frying pan to sautè the onions for about 10 minutes. Add the tomatoes, the cinnamon, the bay leaf, the salt and pepper. Simmer for about 20 minutes, with the pot covered until the sauce sets in and the onions soften.

4. Serve the split peas puree on a platter and pour the sauce over with a spoon. Serve at room temperature.

SPLIT-PEAS BALLS

(serves 6)

Ingredients:

2 cups of Santorini split peas puree

2 tbsps spring onion, finely chopped

1 tsp chopped mint (or parsley),

finely chopped

2 tbsps fine semolina

1 teacup olive oil

Salt and pepper

Preparation:

1. Make the split-peas puree the previous day and refrigerate it for at least 24 hours as soon as it reaches room temperature.

2. The following day transfer the puree into a larger bowl. Add the spring onion, the mint, the semolina, the salt and pepper. Blend using your hands.

3. Mould the mixture into walnut size balls and press each ball gently between your palms. Refrigerate the balls for about an hour.

4. Heat the olive oil in a non-stick frying pan over high heat. Using a perforated spatula, place the balls/burgers in the pan to brown on both sides.

5. When done, place the balls on absorbent paper to drain excess oil.

Serve warm.

ROAST PORK WITH SPLIT PEAS
(serves 6)

Ingredients:	1 tbsp caper
1kg Santorini split peas	1 tsp olive oil
1/2 kg smoke-cured pork (preferably leg)	

Preparation:

1. Having boiled the split peas in water with just a pinch of salt (the caper is already salty), let it stand in the cooking vessel for a while to absorb the liquids well.

2. Cut the pork into small pieces; sauté them lightly in olive oil and drain them.

3. Mix the pork pieces with the split peas. Rinse the capper well under tap water, strain and add it to the mixture.

4. Place it in small casseroles and roast it at 150º C for 20 minutes.

5. Serve with trimmed caper leaves and fresh diced or sliced tomatoes.

BEEF OR CHICKEN "YIOUVETSI"
(serves 8-10)

Ingredients:	pasta)
1 1/2 kilo beef (shoulder – blade)	1 medium onion, quartered
or pork or 1 whole chicken	1 tbs, olive oil
2 large ripe tomatoes,	1 tbs, butter
sliced 1-2 cm thick	Salt Pepper
1 packet kritharaki (barley shaped	Grated cheese

Preparation:

1. Rinse meat under cold, running water and cut into large pieces. Place in lidded clay pot. Pour olive oil and two cups water over meat and arrange sliced tomatoes over top. Cover and bake in center of oven at 200º C for 45-50 minutes. Lower heat to 180º C and cook for one hour more.

2. When meat is cooked, boil pasta with onion for 5 minutes. Drain and add butter. Stir well so that pasta is coated. Season lightly with salt and pepper.

3. Open pot pour pasta around meat. Lightly season meat with salt and pepper. Cover and return to oven. Bake at 200º C for 8 minutes. Turn off heat and let pot stand in hot oven for 20 minutes. Add grated cheese before serving.

RABBIT TIRAVGOULO

(serves 6)

Ingredients:

1kg rabbit, chopped up to small pieces

1 medium-sized onion, finely chopped

1 clove garlic, finely chopped

1 tbsp fresh butter

1 tsp flour

1 glass red wine

2 bay leaves

2 eggs

3/4 cup hard cheese, grated

(preferably kefalotiri)

Preparation:

1. Sauté the onion and butter in a deep, heavy bottom pot until the onions get slightly brown. Stir in the flour using a wooden spoon and add the chopped pieces of rabbit.

2. When the meat starts to brown, add the bay leaves, a pinch of salt, the wine and $1/2$ cup of water. Simmer for 30 –40 minutes with the pot covered.

3. Check if the rabbit is done using a fork. If the rabbit is tender, lower the heat to simmer for a while. Wire-whisk the eggs in a large bowl, adding spoon-by-spoon $1^{1}/_{2}$ cups of stock from the pot.

4. Finally, add the grated cheese and a pinch of pepper in the bowl, stir and pour the mixture in the pot. Bring the meal to boil for about 4-5 minutes. Serve the Rabbit "Tiravgoulo" warm.

"KAKAVIA" (SHORE DINNER)
(serves 6)

Ingredients:
2 teacups extra virgin olive oil
4 large onions, finely chopped
1 large potato, cubed (optional)
1/3 teacup vinegar, from red wine
1kg fish suitable for soup
(gurnard, perch, dorado or bogue)
Salt
Fresh lemon juice (optional)

Preparation:
1. Heat the olive oil in a large pot over moderate heat and add the onions. Cover the pot, lower the heat, and leave the onions to steam in the oil for about 15 minutes until they get very soft. Add the vinegar. After about 1 minute, when the vinegar will have evaporated, layer the fish pieces in the pot, starting with the larger ones first. Sprinkle each layer with a little salt. Add water and top the fish by 2,5 cm. Cover the pot and cook the shore dinner at moderate heat, until the fish pieces are tender when tested with a fork.
2. Before serving, transfer the fish from the pot to a large platter. You could sprinkle them with olive oil and lemon juice. Serve the stock in individual bowls or in deep dishes with the fish pieces.

COD FISH "BRANDATHA"

(6 servings)

Ingredients:

1 large potato, boiled

3 cloves garlic

2 cups olive oil

5 tbsps strong vinegar

1 fillet of salt cod

2 tbsps tomato paste

Salt

1/2 tsp sugar

Preparation:

1. Cut up the cod into small pieces and let them rest in a large bowl of water to desalt for at least 8 hours. In the meanwhile change the water in the bowl at least 2-3 times.

2. The following day prepare the garlic sauce by placing in a blender bowl the potato (diced), the garlic, 3/4 of a cup live oil and the vinegar. Run the blender to get a thin paste with strong taste.

3. Drain the cod and place it on absorbent kitchen paper to dry.

4. Pour a cup of olive oil in a non-stick frying pan and allow it to heat well. Fry the cod pieces until they get brown on both sides. When the cod pieces are done, remove them using a perforated spatula and place them on a large dish lined with absorbent kitchen paper.

5. In another deep and clean frying pan pour 3 tablespoons of olive oil and once it has heated, pour the tomato paste (previously thinned with 3/4 cup of water, and mixed with the salt and the sugar). This will make your sauce.

6. Let the sauce boil for about 8 minutes. Start adding slowly the sauce whilst stirring it with a wooden spoon until it turns into a homogenous red cream.

7. Place the fried cod pieces in a shallow pyrex dish and pour the garlic sauce over them.

8. Insert the pyrex dish in the oven to bake for 10 minutes 150º C. Serve the «Brandatha» cod warm.

EGGPLANT SALAD WITH OCTOPUS

(serves 6-8)

Ingredients:

4-5 eggplants (white species, preferably)

2 medium-sized tomatoes, cubed

2 spring onions, chopped

1 tablespoon parsley, finely chopped

1 clove garlic

3-4 tablespoons olive oil

1 tablespoon vinegar

salt

THE OCTOPUS

1 octopus (800gr to 1kg): boiled and chopped

2 tablespoons olive oil

2 tablespoons vinegar

a shot of oregano

salt & pepper

Preparation:

1. Use a fork to pierce the eggplants 2-3 times and place them in salted water to "remove" bitter taste.

2. Drain eggplants and arrange them on oven grate to grill until their skin is soft.

3. Peel skin carefully and scoop out their flesh in a bowl. Add the garlic (mashed), the olive oil, the vinegar and a little salt. Use a fork to mix all ingredients in the bowl.

4. Transfer and spread the eggplant salad on a platter. Use a spoon to make space in the middle of the salad to place the octopus. Sprinkle with a little parsley and serve at room temperature.

FISH ROE SALAD

Served in 2 little bowls

Ingredients:

2 tablespoons roe (white or red)
$^1/_2$ bread (the crumbs)

$^1/_2$ cup virgin olive oil
1 clove garlic
1 lemon, the juice of

Preparation:

1. Soak the breadcrumbs in water and squeeze them in your hands to strain them completely. Put the crumbs in a blender, add the garlic cloves, the roe and start blending the mixture at medium speed. Add the olive oil and lemon juice little by little, alternating between the two, to get a homogenous thin paste. Serve in two little bowls.

OCTOPUS IN WINE (snack)

(serves 8-10)

Ingredients:

1 kg octopus
$^1/_2$ water glass olive oil

1 cup red wine
salt, pepper

Preparation:

1. Clean and wash the octopus very well and slice it to small pieces. If the octopus is fresh, you need to beat, pound and rub it on a rough surface from 20-30 minutes to soften it. Alternatively, you may put it in a freezer for 24 hours.

2. Put the octopus pieces in a shallow, non-stick frying pan to simmer them in their juices at 100° C for 10 minutes.

3. When the octopus has absorbed all of its juice, add two glasses of water and the olive oil.

4. While cooking, test tenderness using a fork. Having established that the octopus is almost done, gradually add the wine and stir at the same time, to make the sauce. Serve warm.

HONEY AND ALMOND FILLED ROLLS

(15-20 small rolls)

Ingredients:	1 tsp soda
For the dough	3 tbsps brandy
$^1/_2$ kg unsalted butter	1 $^1/_2$ kg white flour
$^1/_2$ kg sugar	
6 eggs	For the filling:
Juice from 2 large oranges	$^1/_2$ kg ground sesame
the grated rind from a 1 large lemon	150 gr crashed almonds
1 tsp cinnamon	600 gr honey
$^1/_2$ tsp clove (powder)	1 tsp cinnamon
1 tsp baking powder	1 egg white - meringue

Preparation:

1. Prepare the dough: Beat the butter with the sugar in a bowl or mixer until the mixture turns white. Add all the eggs one by one, but save one egg-white which you will need for the filling. Then add all the spices, the orange, the soda, the brandy, the baking powder and half the flour quantity.

2. Mix all the ingredients to get a smooth mixture and gradually add the remaining flour, until the dough turns homogenous and soft. Cover it up with a cotton towel and let it rise to double in volume – about an hour.

3. For the filling: place all filling ingredients in a bowl and mix them together well using your hands. Next, cut pieces of dough the size of a small peach and shape them into strings 10-15 cm long, 4-5 cm wide. Flatten strings by hand and place the filling lengthwise. Fold the long side to secure the filling in the dough and bend in the center to shape rolls. Wet the edges slightly and secure the joint by sticking a clove.

4. Place the rolls on a slightly buttered pan and bake them at 180o C for 45-50 minutes. Leave them to cool down and then serve.

"KATSIA"
HALLOWEEN SWEET
(approximately 40 pieces)

Ingredients:

Phyllo:
1 kg white flour
4 tbsps olive oil
3-4 tbsps ouzo or raki
1 pinch salt

Filling:
1 kg sweet myzithra or ricotta
$1/2$ kg roasted sesame
$1/2$ tsp cinnamon
$1/2$ tsp clove (powder) or nutmeg
2 eggs
1 tsp grated orange rind
Juice from $1/2$ orange
1 teacup olive oil (for frying)

Preparation:

1. To prepare the filling, place the myzithra in a bowl or mixer and stir/run until it crumbles to pieces. Pound the sesame and mix it with the myzithra. Then mix all the ingredients together, or run the mixer.

2. Pour the flour into a bowl and make a well in the center, where you pour in the olive oil, the ouzo or the raki, the salt and half a teacup of warm water.

3. Start kneading the dough, gradually adding water if necessary, until the dough becomes soft and tender. Cover dough with a cotton towel to rest for about 10-15 minutes.

4. Roll out phyllos, 1 cm thick, and cut out circular discs approximately 3-4 cm in diameter. Place a tablespoon of filling in the center and fold to crescent shape. Use a fork (back side) and press the half-moon perimeter to secure the filling well.

5. Fry them in hot olive oil. Take them out using a perforated spatula and place them on absorbent kitchen paper to drain. Serve them hot or warm with honey on top.

TO KOUFETO
(for 1 large jar)

Ingredients:	1 cup
1kg pumpkin (white species prefera-bly)	1 cup blanched almonds cut in half longitudinally
$^1/_2$ kg sugar	$^1/_2$ cup water
$^1/_2$ kg honey	the juice from a small lemon

Preparation:

1. Cut the pumpkin to slices as you would potatoes for French fries, then rinse, transfer to a strainer and let them drain well.

2. Bring the water, sugar and honey to the boil in a pot. Add the pumpkin slices and cook over high heat to make the syrup. Skim as necessary.

3. When the syrup is ready, add the almonds and the lemon juice. Remove from heat and let the syrup stand to cool down, then transfer the dessert in large jars.

"KOPANIA"
(20-25 pieces)

Ingredients:	2 teacups red currants
2 teacups of sesame	2-6 tbsps water
2 barley rusks	

Preparation:

1. Roast the sesame seeds in a dry frying pan over low heat, stirring constantly so that the seeds don't burn, until they obtain a nice, slightly golden color (approx. 2-4 minutes). Transfer them into a vessel and let them stand to cool down.

2. Place half the sesame quantity in a large mortar and crush them. Break the rusks into pieces, gradually adding them in the mortar to reduce them to powder. Add the red currants and keep on pounding until the mixture turns to paste. You may need to add a couple of tablespoons of water, to get the right texture.

3. You can do the same using a blender (adjust a metallic blade). First, blend half the ses-ame quantity then gradually add the barley rusks (first cut to small pieces) to reduce all to powder. Remove the mixture from the blender, add the red currants and run the blender to turn them into a thick and moist paste. Slowly add the sesame-rusks (powder) and run the blender to get a homogenous mixture. You may need to add a little water to get the right texture. Transfer the entire mixture into a bowl.

4. Use a tablespoon to collect mixture; shape each tablespoon quantity into a small ball and roll ball into a small cylinder over the remaining sesame and serve. If wrapped in grease paper, the cookies can be placed in jars and stored in a cool and dry place for a long time.

MELITINIA
(30 – 40 pieces)

Ingredients:

For the dough:

1 kg of all-purpose flour

50 gr butter

a pinch of salt

Water

For the filling:

1 kg unsalted myzithra

1 kg sugar

250 gr self-rising flour

3-4 eggs

20 gr Chios Mastic, crushed and sifted

little vanilla powder

Preparation:

1. Mix all the ingredients for the dough and knead it but not too soft. Leave dough to rest for about 20 minutes.

2. Roll out dough into fine sheets and cut out 4-5cm discs using a cookie cutter. Shape a cavity in the discs to spoon in the filling.

3. To make the filling: mix the myzithra and the sugar; add the flour and the whisked eggs, the mastic and the vanilla. Mix well until you get a thick and smooth mixture.

4. Fill the dough cavities with a tablespoonful of filling. Place the Melitinia in a buttered pan and bake them for approximately 40 minutes at 180° C until they get a nice golden color.

SANTORINI PUDDING

(serves 10)

Ingredients:	For the sauce:
2 lt fresh milk	200 ml sweet, black wine or 1
2 cups fine semolina	bottle of Santorini Vinsanto
100 gr fresh butter	1 glass sugar
320 gr. sugar*	$^1/_2$ tsp ground cinnamon
4 eggs	
1 tsp ground cinnamon	

Preparation:

1. Wire-whisk the eggs in a large bowl. Add the milk and butter (at room temperature), the semolina and the cinnamon. Stir contents to mix them well.

2. Pour the mixture into a round greased pan (4-5cm diam., 5-6 cm height), and place it in a larger pan with water (ben mari) and into the oven.

3. Cook the pudding at 200° C for approximately an hour. In the meantime boil the sugar with the wine until the sauce sets.

4. Let the pudding cool off and cut it into small, square pieces. Serve each piece of pudding pouring a spoon of wine sauce on top.

* If you use a sweet wine like Vinsanto or Mavrodaphne, reduce the amount of sugar in the ingredients.

"AMIGDALOTO"
(Traditional sweet for wedding celebrations)

(20-30 pieces)

Ingredients:	400 gr white sugar
1 kg shelled and blanched almonds	150 gr egg whites

Preparation:

1. Use a blender to reduce almonds to powder. Add the rest of the ingredients and run blender to get firm dough.

2. Pick $^1/_2$ tablespoons of dough approximately and mould into balls. Flatten balls a little to shape round dough discs (2-3 cm in diam., 1 cm thick or the size of chocolate chip cookies) and place discs onto a greased cookie sheet.

3. Stick two almonds in the center of every dough disc and bake them in the oven at 140°C for 40 minutes. Remove them from the cookie sheet when at room temperature.

KOLOKYTHERI

(for 20-25 servings)

Ingredients:

For the phyllo

6 teacups all-purpose flour

2 tbsps "tsipouro"

a pinch of salt

1 tbsp soft butter or olive oil

1 1/2 teacups water (approximately)

* If you want, you can use 1 packet of traditional phyllo.

For the filling

1 1/2 kg pumpkin

1/2 kg fresh, unsalted myzithra or sweet anthotiro (ricotta)

2-3 eggs

1/2 tsp pepper

3 teacups sugar

3 tbsps cinnamon

2 teacups honey

2 teacups flour (approximately)

Preparation:

1. Mix all the phyllo ingredients and knead to make dough which you let rest at a cool place for an hour.

2. In the meantime, prepare the filling: Clean the pumpkin and grate it using an onion grater. Transfer the grated pumpkin in a strainer to drain well.

3. Blend the myzithra in a vegetable mill and add the sugar, the eggs (slightly beaten), the cinnamon and the pumpkin. Pour in the flour, half the honey quantity and stir vigorously.

4. Roll out the dough to a thin phyllo and use it to line a round, greased baking pan (approximately 40 cm in diameter). If you have purchased a packet of phyllo, use 2-3 sheets to line the bottom of the pan.

5. Pour the filling over the phyllo and bring in the edges to form a kind of garland. Preheat the oven at 250° C to bake the pie for about 30 minutes.

6. Remove the pie from the oven; pour the remaining honey on top and continue baking at 190° C for one more hour. Let the pie cool down before serving.

RUSKS WITH SAFFRON
(48 rusks)

Ingredients:
12-14 teacups flour for bread making
2 sachets yeast
4 $^1/_2$ teacups warm water
$^1/_2$ -1 tsp saffron
$^1/_2$ tsp salt
$^3/_4$ teacup unsalted, soft butter

1 $^1/_2$ teacups sugar
5 large eggs
1 tbsp pounded fennel seeds
1 yolk of a large egg whisked in 2 tbsps milk and 1 tbsp water
2 tbsps sesame to sprinkle

Preparation:

1. Use a medium-sized bowl to mix 2 teacups of flour with the yeast and add $^1/_2$ teacup warm water. First stir to mix the contents of the bowl then start kneading to get smooth dough. Cover the dough with a towel and let it rest in a warm and dry place for either 8 hours or overnight.

2. Put the saffron in a large cup and add 1 cup of warm water. Cover the large cup with a towel and let the saffron soak for several hours.

3. Mix 10 cups from the remaining flour with the salt in a large bowl and make a large well (more like a crater) in the middle. Crumble the yeast and place the pieces in the well and pour in the water with the saffron. Use a bowl to whisk in the butter with the sugar to get a soft mass and then whisk in the eggs, one at a time, until you get a creamy mixture. Pour this mixture into the well.

4. Have 2 $^1/_2$ teacups of warm water standing by. Start mixing and kneading the flour mixture with your hands, adding water as you go along until you get smooth dough. Add the fennel seeds. (Alternatively, you can do the same in a blender using the dough mixing blades). Knead until the dough becomes smooth and soft, adding flour if necessary.

5. Grease four baking tins 30 cm long. Separate the dough into 4 equal balls giving each the shape of a long loaf. Place the loaves in the baking tins. With a dough cutter or a knife, score each loaf at 2,5cm distances, where you will later cut the loaves to slices. Cover the loaves and let them rest in a warm and dry place for approximately 2 hours to rise.

6. Preheat the oven at 200º C. Brush each loaf with whisked egg and sprinkle with sesame. Bake the loaves for 45 min. approx., until they get slightly golden on top. Remove loaves from the oven and place them on grates to cool down. Slice loaves where pre-scored and place the slices flat on grease paper. Lower the temperature to 100º C and bake the rusks until they get really hard (approx. 3 hours). Remove from the oven and let slices cool off completely. Store slices in biscuit bins. They can be preserved for a long time.

TOP TRADITIONAL PRODUCTS AND WHERE YOU CAN FIND THEM

TROULAKIS - TRADITIONAL PRODUCTS "HELIOTROPIO":

This is a shop decorated with gusto and stocked with fresh and processed products of Santorini: white aubergines, cherry tomatoes, barley rusks, sun-dried cherry tomatoes, capers, melitinia, local and national wine.
Location: on the road from Fera to Pyrgos.
Tel.: 22860-27047

UNION OF ASSOCIATIONS OF THERAIC PRODUCTS

In addition to select wine varieties, the Wines-Tourism Centre has set up a special hall where visitors can find collector's vials for storing wine, books and other items relating to wine as well as a display of other products of Thera, e.g. split peas, cherry tomatoes, capers, blackberry syrup, etc.
Address: Pyrgos Santorini, 847 00,
Tel: (22860) 22596, 25128, 25420, fax (22860) 23137

OPEN AIR MARKET: Not far from the main square of Thera a small open market operates once a week.
There you can find all kinds of produce: lentil, green/white aubergines, vegetable marrows, cherry tomatoes and capers.

"ANYDRO"
Organic Cultures of Santorini
Megalohori
Tel. 22860 81820

LOCAL COOKING TUTORING: Mr. Georgios Hatzigiannakis and his wife Evelyn will be happy to initiate you to the secrets of the Santorini kitchen. Their tutoring is an interesting guide to the fragrant products of the island. Classes are one- or two-day sessions and take place in the tutors' charming restaurant.
Tel.: 22860-22249.

RESTAURANTS

Kyra Katina

This restaurant is located in the picturesque inlet of Oea, with deep blue crystal clear waters and imposing volcanic rocks. The owner, Mrs Katina (Kyra Katina) is an expert in cooking fresh fish, lobster-spaghetti, salads, split-peas puree, fried tomato-balls and calamari on the grill.
Location: Amoudi
Tel: 22860 71260
Open: daily from April to October, noon and evening

Koukoumvalos

This is a very interesting restaurant as it combines international cooking skills with local products. The resulting dishes are colorful and tasty, e.g. tantalizing crayfishes' tails in white sauce, piquant ginger and aniseed ouzo. The restaurant has received the "Golden Cap" award.
International cuisine
Tel. 22860 23807
Open: daily from April to October, noon and evening

Ammos

Relaxation in Greece is part and parcel with "high spirited" drinks. In this restaurant the recipe for relaxation is ouzo combined with dry-salted fish cooked by the owner himself. Other items on the menu are: fried vegetable balls made from split-peas puree, dill and spring onions; or marrows and fresh tomatoes as main ingredients.
This is a fish tavern.
Location: Fera, 12 km
Tel: 22860 81819
Open: daily from May to September, noon and evening

Nikolas

This restaurant offers simple preparations from fresh and simple ingredients. Mr. Thomas Likourinos is very skillful in combining these ingredients into delectable snacks

and dishes: fried small fish, stewed cuttlefish in wine, juicy lamb with oregano, etc.
Tavern - casserole dishes.
Location: Erythros Stavros.
Tel: 22860-24550
Open: daily all year round (excepting Sunday noon), noon and evening

Diktia (Nets)

This is a fish tavern. In the beautifully arranged garden of Michalis Troulakis you will enjoy a wide range of seafood with a view to the deep blue sea of the Aegean. The restaurant offers juicy gurnard on the grill, octopus tentacles on the grill, grouper cooked in sea-water and olive oil, a colorful salad which, among other ingredients, includes rocket and Santorini cherry tomatoes. The spaghetti with shrimps and other seafood is exquisite.

The owner is from the island of Crete and never fails to remind this with an item on the menu: snails fried in rosemary.
Tel.: 22860-82918
Open: daily from March to November, noon and evening

"1800"

This restaurant is housed in a renovated neoclassical building, offering a warm atmosphere, the result of elegant wood furniture, featuring also a beautiful garden. This rather classy context combines with a range of gastronomic temptations. The menu includes dishes made from fresh Mediterranean products which the chef uses in a creative way to balance tastes and aromas. This restaurant will surprise you in a pleasant way.
Mediterranean cuisine.
Tel. 22860-71485
Open: daily from April to October, noon and evening.

Kyra Rosa

Most of the menu items come under the classic title "mama's cooking". The preparations of Mrs. Rosa are reminiscent of Sunday lunch, when families gather to enjoy home cooking. This restaurant specializes in casserole dishes, rabbit stew, pilaf with wild birds, cottage sausages stuffed with rice and chopped liver, refreshing salads, and meat on the grill. Also, the French fries are delicious.
Location: Vourvoulos (4 km from Fera)
Open: daily all year round, noon and evening

Selini

The tireless and ingenious, always smiling, Mr. Georgios Hatzigiannakis and his wife Evelyn, will be your hosts in their "volcanic cuisine"!! Their style of cooking is dedicated to traditional materials offering distinctive tastes that encourage you to become a regular patron - a decision enhanced by the location of the restaurant. We recommend the split-peas puree which is served with urchins' roe and baby artichokes. You will also find delicious the fish soup made from grouper, and ravioli topped with sour myzithra. The

same is true for the tender lamb with aubergines.
For desert we recommend sweet myzithra with preserve made from capers and cherry tomatoes.
This restaurant offers Greek and Mediterranean cuisine
Tel.: 22860-22249
Open: from April to October